C O S M O G O N Y *O F*

AN E V E N T

script for a spy film at Sasso Saraceno

by
Francesco Mangone

translated by
Pasquale Verdicchio

PARENTHESES WRITING SERIES
1988

COSMOGONY OF AN EVENT

Time of narration: a pure Midnight in July.
Lighting: large moon, its shining scales on the tar-like sea.
Music: slow rhythm of a Beguine.
Sounds: whispering voices heard as always.

Characters

Marius: painter and such, owner of the Terrace
                     "Sasso Saraceno" — aesthetic factors will later
                     render him Zagreo the hyperboreal —

Three poets: young and not well defined;

The spy: actually a mask, a hypothetical X;

Franz: mute waiter, will abuse the corpses before
                     throwing them into the sea;

Corybants: enrapturing fumes, chasing Franz.

The action is born of gesture, which redescends
the steps of ink in the perspective of the white page.
Scattered flashes at intervals from the cones of shadow.
The scene is desert-like ... a polar desert.
A summer terrace.
The furnishings are arranged in a provisional manner, empty,
apparent ... in anticipation of an arrival — the epopteia
of the Eleusian rites; whenever it may happen — always
a little further or a little nearer — the conscience arrives
a fraction late ... Every human word is banished ...
the absolute depth of doubt, or mystery, reigns.

1
(almost a premise)

. . . Valhalla
gazing again wave to wave
                the sonority
concave . . . of rebelling tufts
— the monochordal emptiness of vowels —
                . . . spoke of himself
in unbecoming terms
                Marius listened
astounded selling in a few frames
the furrows of roaring waves
                — the consonants —

2
(almost an invocation)

oh!   the hour Lola
the water of Violet Moon
to such fate the Terrace prepares
like balconies
        on the wattles
        the buzz / the murmur
the cutting felids
        the young age
the best greenery that he readies for the Bello
        — his is the world —
        at Maraviglia
        that is
the game between you ... el moto ... whoops!
        ... careful!
slightly the risk of being Mute
because from Lola
        I want the sun understand ...
        do you?! ...

3

(meanwhile beach-boys are going for a stroll)

Marius: wise gentlemen the establishment
             is what it appears to be to any one of you
                         nothing more than this . . .
             odalisques in the smoke of the wave
             faint full of you . . .
                         . . . ready to cast off its moorings
                         among the bodies hairs of water
             while from the shadow . . . cargoes on the route
             between Shabadane and
                         Crotone . . . unloads the opium
                         at night . . .
             . . . this is the space spoken by my paintings!
             the event imitates . . . shameful
                         only
             only for so little . . . net sum of
                         expenses between
                         frame and passe-partout

4

(young poets clinking green-cool-drinks)

The poet: . . . to stop here is a game of goose
                    closer
                    the wave of wave
             . . . you like it stretched out among the canes
             naked adolescents
                    flexed in the water
             to experiment   contemporaries . . .
                    seems . . . appears . . . finally!
             shadow of the moon in excess
             . . . I did not dare to say on the shores . . .
                    I respected of you with me its
             cadute-ute-te   the wisterias
                    slightly violated me   a time
                    of ochre
             one stroke of the wing and away . . .

5

the spy: where the eye arrives narrating
                    it unveils
            organizes possession or hopes!
            confusing moving toward — where?
                    . . . constrained fabulating
            to retrace paths   little spouts
            or spheres incisions fine
                    among the limes   stones among
            the tables the surprise
                                chewing
            the waiting . . . to be whence one is caught
                    passing over the panes
                    the furtive strained in vain
            the hip it poses le mer reposes
                              — constrained sense —
            slightly glancing a spy (the spy) between
            the corner of the eyes and the profile of a
                    secret . . . sigh . . . is spied!
            he has a nose . . . of course he has   by god!
                    if he has a nose . . .

6

III poet: the ardour that you take
Fanes!
the acrid ardour of certain gold
      of your nights in the measure
of marine plants
      while you flare at the cold
hips
columns of fugitive moons!

II poet: embraces
compressed precise perplexed . . .
— under the lights on the chairs —

I poet: that wind rustle?
the only shiver . . . from below
a hairy stomach . . . fleeting
bird . . .

III poet: good Lord!

*(sudden darkness on the set, three gunshots
in quick succession; screams, confusion;
slowly things return to normal)*

7

*(Franz, aided by the confusion, takes advantage of
the still warm corpses; then, lacerated by the Corybants,
the parts are pushed into the current of a tar-like sea)*

(Marius: disrobing, shows the customers his divine origins.)

Zagreo: poets lost
to the waves among valences — bodies of birches —
   polyps in the wind
want germinates from the flesh of he who appears
   displays — shines
   from the only possible reality
Total
   or on the other hand in a couple
mortal abyss of the enigma!
   . . . rows of grape vines
   up to the slopes of Mount Lotros
mute
the statues of salt throws open the water now here
   violating kind of entelechy
   extreme walks the invasion
between pauses stated
   to the being . . .   of being as such . . .
   ( )   the sea . . .

8

(. . . from the enclosure at Eleusis; the unsayable for
our techno-logical Time

for Rocco Guaragna

Corybants: — the opposites were the Beginning!

      — penetrating the unlimited into the limited
       (the infinitely empty in the circle of the
       finite) the multiple of the world generates
       itself

      — while from the Shadow Harmony
       organizes in walks the opposites:
       spheres and concordant lines

      — therefore intuitions are their essence,
       that move themselves backwards

      — supported, for all Time, by
       Fanes   Central Fire
       (rotating system in itself): Ap/Pearance

      — supermen and divine folly busily
       playing with consonants and vowels

     . . .   .

      — but even before the Beginning: the Unsaid!

9

the spy: oh . . . by god . . . the stumbling block?!

      — the flashing indifferent
          a god's thunderbolt! —

          . . . all the way down . . . to the roots
          of the scream
to the shadow's net excision . . .

      — the spy having searched for the Event had
          proposed it
          to the disordered room
someone hoped
or even wound
to fight for his certainties . . . —

          . . . the paradigms . . .

(inhabiting the Uninhabited the measures
exchanged their affinities, established
by Game and Necessity in search of Time)

10

(. . . and all is played as with the Greek
term: physis)

. . . the unforeseen!!
                        there under the lights
rattling
advancing slowly
among retreating
herons . . .   the aperitifs
                          poured
on one side . . . the cooked fish
le maquillage
                          le doux perlage . . .
. . . from shore
to shore . . .   tong-like
we advance or Franz jaw of
Prussian servant
                          enjoyed glasses
from behind   by now supposed
                          by now proposed
                          by now the advent
(and everyone clapped their hands   their hands
 everyone clapped)

                — nature rules! —

Final Considerations

Logical phase

the *three poets* dissolved
on the line of the dialogue disposed
themselves to the return that leads
to things . . .
an infinity of pathways . . .

the spy moving from the inadequacy
of his eye — that is techno-logical power —
is induced to express himself ulteriorly
in order to heal the equilibrium . . .

Problem: to realize the hypothetical X: the story

Mythical Phase

Marius-Zagreo: Will of metaphysical will
that commands the world of
Appearance ("Apollonian" vertex)

Franz and Corybants: Dionysian procession
ravager of appearance (orgiastic and dissolute
depth of folly)